S0-BOR-011

How to draw pets and small animals

Christine Smith

TRODDY BOOKS

Materials

It's easier to draw with good materials so get the best you can. Pencils with an 'H' at the end are hard and not good for drawings. An 'HB' is medium and good for your first rough drawings. Later, try a 'B' pencil. They are velvety, soft and especially nice to draw with.

This pencil sharpener is good because it keeps all the shavings inside its little container.

If you use thin paper you can place this over your first rough drawing and make a clean finished drawing, leaving out the guide lines.

You'll need a soft eraser for getting rid of mistakes. To colour the drawing, try using felt pens, water colours, crayons or coloured pencils to find what suits you best.

Shapes

Before you start the drawings in the book, practise the above shapes. Draw them over and over again until you get nice round circles and good smooth ovals. All the drawings in the book are made from these easy shapes. Try making your own animals using circles, squares and triangles.

Colour

Colour mixing is fun whether you are using coloured pencils or paint. Try red and yellow to make orange. Mix blue and yellow to make green. Red and blue will make purple.

An important thing to remember
when you're drawing small animals
is that their heads are quite large
compared with the body.
The difference between a hen and
her chick would look like this...

Look hard at all the small animals
you see, make a note of colours and
special marks. Some artists carry a
small note book and when they see
something interesting they make a
drawing of it for later use.

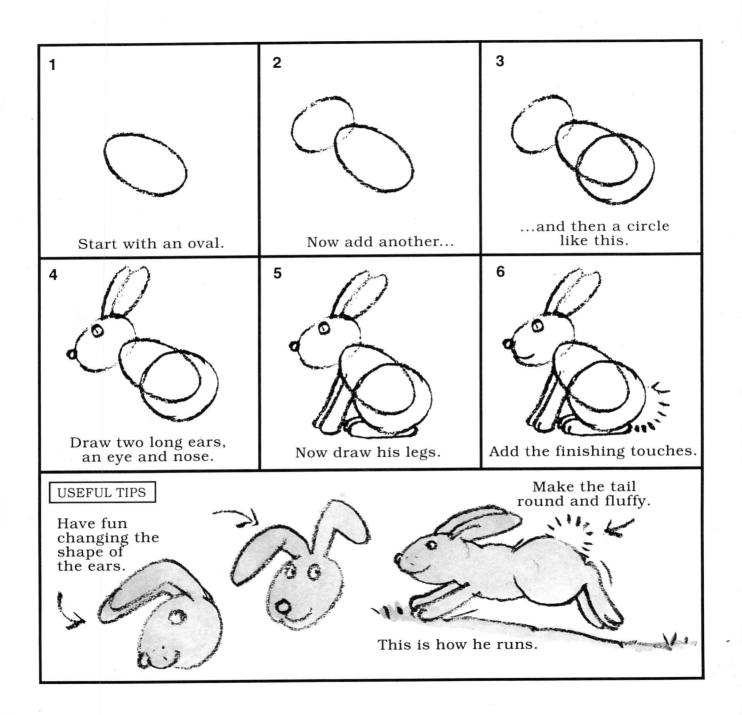

1 Start with an oval.

2 Now add another...

3 ...and then a circle like this.

4 Draw two long ears, an eye and nose.

5 Now draw his legs.

6 Add the finishing touches.

USEFUL TIPS

Have fun changing the shape of the ears.

Make the tail round and fluffy.

This is how he runs.

Rabbit

1 Start with a circle...

2 ...and a smaller one.

3 Now join them to make the neck.

4 Add an eye, a beak and a wing.

5 Draw legs like this.

6 Add the finishing touches.

USEFUL TIPS

Chicks are easy.

Try making your chicken peck grain.

Put in the feathers like this.

Chicken

1 Start with an oval.

2 Draw front legs like this.

3 Add ears and a body...

4 ...eyes and a nose...

5 ...cheeks and a tail.

6 Add the finishing touches.

USEFUL TIPS

Make changes by putting the eye dots in different places.

Make the paws more rounded like this.

Trace the outline of your first drawing to make a back view.

Kitten

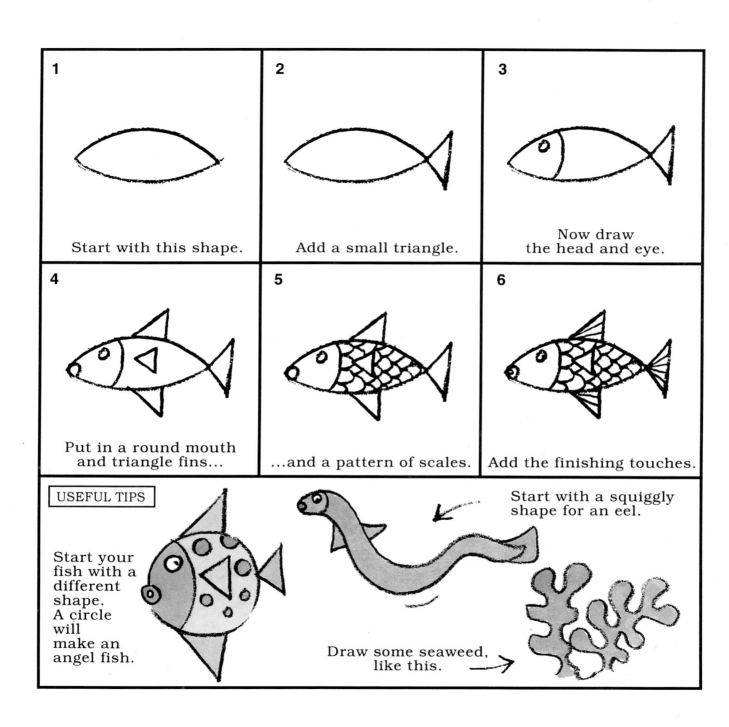

1 Start with this shape.

2 Add a small triangle.

3 Now draw the head and eye.

4 Put in a round mouth and triangle fins...

5 ...and a pattern of scales.

6 Add the finishing touches.

USEFUL TIPS

Start your fish with a different shape. A circle will make an angel fish.

Start with a squiggly shape for an eel.

Draw some seaweed, like this.

Fish

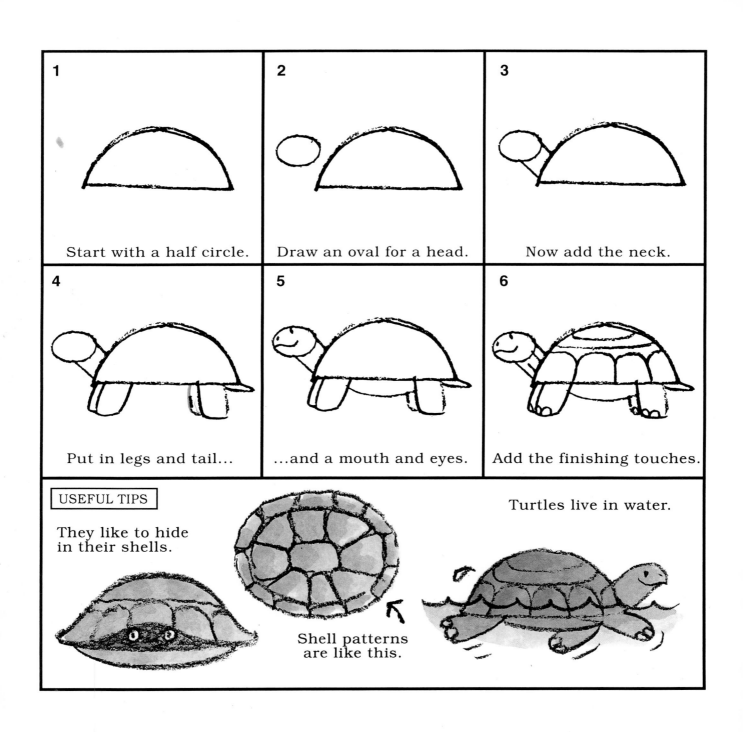

1 Start with a half circle.

2 Draw an oval for a head.

3 Now add the neck.

4 Put in legs and tail...

5 ...and a mouth and eyes.

6 Add the finishing touches.

USEFUL TIPS

They like to hide in their shells.

Shell patterns are like this.

Turtles live in water.

Tortoise

1

Draw a circle and a smaller one, then join them up like this.

2

Do the same again for the body.

3

Now join them like this.

4

Add ears and an eye...

5

...and draw long legs.

6

Add the finishing touches.

USEFUL TIPS

As you get better at drawing, try the hooves like this.

Grazing.

The legs move like this when running.

Foal

1 Start with an oval.

2 Add a circle at one end.

3 Draw another circle for his snout.

4 Add eyes, ears...

5 ...legs and a curly tail.

6 Add the finishing touches.

USEFUL TIPS

Babies have smaller bodies.

Try a side face like this.

Pig

1 Start with a circle.

2 Add a larger half circle...

3 ...a beak and tail.

4 Draw the legs like this.

5 Add an eye and wing.

6 Add the finishing touches.

USEFUL TIPS

Try the wings like this to make the bird fly.

Perch like this.

This one is landing on the ground.

Bird

1

Start with two ovals.

2

Now another for the body.

3

Draw the nose and mouth.

4

Add the ears and eyes.

5

Draw four little legs.

6

Add the finishing touches.

USEFUL TIPS

Bigger eyes
for more
expression.

Try a few spots.

Sitting down.

Puppy

We hope you enjoyed learning to draw

pets and small animals

Painter and illustrator, Christine Smith lives and
works in a charming old farmhouse in the south of
England. Her young children and their collection of
pets and stray animals add to her ever-growing
household and provide endless material and
inspiration for her delightful books.